D1017162

...rit is by definition an immaterial essence. It has been called *clar...*
..., the soul; life force; the divine self, the true self and more recentl...
...ner child. Nevertheless there is broad agreement that the spirit exist...
... distinct from the body and from the mind. In our hearts, we all kno...
...e are spirits and that our body is our vessel as we travel through life...
... earth. When something or someone speaks to us and reaches u...
..., it reaches our very soul, our true inner self. Despite the efforts...

sac-
ruc-
l our
This
ence
cur
ok is
lding
deci-
spirit
; the
inner
id is
that
'e our
s us
forts
sac-
ruc-

f our genes, we know, without a doubt that above and beyond our
al self there is our spirit, which is our true and lasting self. This
s about spirit. It is about the most noble and fundamental essence
man being and life on earth. For life to exist, for creation to occur
ange to manifest itself, it must be endowed with spirit. This book is
bout you. The real you. The creative, thinking, dreaming, building

he spirit is by definition an immaterial essence. It has been called
Vital", the soul; life force; the divine self, the true self and more rec
he inner child. Nevertheless there is broad agreement that the spirit
and is distinct from the body and from the mind. In our hearts,
now that we are spirits and that our body is our vessel as we
hrough life on this earth. When something or someone speaks to us

ea
he
um
he
eye
self
al e
o o
pool
nil
deci
spir
Vits
he
and
kno
hro
rea
the
hum

he structure of our genes, we know, without a doubt that above
beyond our material self there is our spirit, which is our true and
self. This book is about spirit. It is about the most noble and funda
tal essence of human being and life on earth. For life to exist, for cr
to occur; for change to manifest itself, it must be endowed with spiri
book is also about you. The real you. The creative thinking; dre

WAY
OF THE
SPIRIT

This book belongs to

_____

© 2000 Modus Vivendi Publishing Inc.
All rights reserved.

Published by:
Modus Vivendi Publishing Inc.
3859 Laurentian Autoroute
Laval, Quebec
Canada H7L 3H7
or
2565 Broadway, Suite 161
New York, New York 10025

Cover: Marc Alain

Picture Credits: © 1997 Wood River Gallery and SuperStock

Legal Deposit: 3rd Quarter, 2000
National Library of Canada

Canadian Cataloguing in Publication Data
Alain, Marc
    Way of the Spirit
    (Heartfelt Series)
    ISBN: 2-89523-026-9
    1. Spirituality. 2. Spirituality – Pictorial works.
    I. Title. II. Series
BV4509.5.D4713 2000   291.4   C00941185-2

Canada We acknowledge the financial support of the Government
of Canada through the Book Publishing Industry Development
Program (BPIDP) for our publishing activities.

WAY
OF THE
SPIRIT

Marc Alain

MV Publishing

"Beware not to decorate your house more than your own soul; give your care to the spirit, your true home."

Jean Hus

The spirit is by definition an immaterial essence. It has been called the life force, the soul, the divine self, the true self and more recently the inner child. Nevertheless there is broad agreement that the spirit exists and is distinct from the body and from the mind. In our hearts, we all know that we are spirits and that our body is our vessel as we travel through life on this Earth. When something or someone speaks to us and reaches us deeply, it reaches our very soul, our true inner self.

Despite the efforts made by the psychiatric and medical communities to explain human reaction and emotion in terms of chemical reactions in the brain or in the structure of our genes, we know without a doubt that above and beyond our material self there is our spirit, which is our true and lasting self.

This book is about spirit. It is about the most noble and fundamental essence of human being and life on Earth. For life to exist, for creation to occur, for change to manifest itself, it must be endowed with spirit. This book is also about you, the real you, the creative, thinking, dreaming, building and feeling you. It is about your consciousness your values and the decisions that shape your life and relationships while you are here on Earth.

Marc Alain

All the Colors

As I gaze upon you
Like a fiery sunset
Eyes filled with admiration
I see all the colors of your beautiful soul

As I embrace you
Like a brush on canvas
Hands firm yet gentle
I feel all the colors of your wonderful soul

As I love you
Like the sunshine loves the flowers
Heart filled with radiant warmth
I inherit the colors of your powerful soul

As I dream of you
Like a child in his mothers arms
Spirit floating free
I swim in the color of your soul

M. A.

> "The work of the mind resembles digging a well; troubled waters eventually give way to clarity."
>
> Chinese Proverb

Sarah was only three when my wife Emily and I split up. The breakup was incredibly painful for me. For what seemed to be the better part of a year, I was in a state of confusion. I realized that I had done things to bring about the end of the relationship — and had even hoped that the relationship would come to an end. However, I had not foreseen the impact the breakup would have on me. It cut through me like a mill saw through a tree.

I saw that Emily had been a part of me. And now, I wandered around in a kind of semi-conscious haze, going through the motions at work, making as if it were business as usual. I began to see that certain things were more important than others: Relationships are more important than material belongings; being happy is more important than success in business; your family and friends are more important than the car you drive and the kind of shoes you wear.

I can tell you that I have never defined myself as a religious or spiritual man. But through this heavy period, I found that I had to pray a lot. My prayers were simple. I asked God to help me through this very difficult time. I asked him to protect my family and friends. I asked him to help me to forgive, to forgive myself for all the wrongs I had committed and to forgive Emily, whom I still had anger toward.

Over the weeks and months I prayed, I could feel a heavy weight lifting from my heart. I slowly began to take pleasure in the simple things in life, like preparing and having a good meal with my daughter. One day, I caught myself laughing heartily at a good joke a friend had emailed me. At that moment, I realized I hadn't laughed like that in months, maybe years. I said to myself, "If there is laugh, there is hope."

Robert B.

"At times we suppress or deny our feelings for fear that those who share our lives will fail to understand them or will refuse to accept them if we verbalize them. But it is only by honoring and recognizing my true feelings that I can achieve emotional recovery, move ahead and grow."

Sue Patton Thoele

When I was a child in Catholic school, I had a mental image of what my soul looked like. I used to picture it like a transparent bone right in the middle of my chest. After all, I had been told that all humans had souls. Our soul was given to us by God and it ultimately belonged to Him. In a way, the soul was a tiny bit of God in all of us. I was also told that if I committed a sin, my soul would be blemished. I would see my transparent bone-soul with a stain on it. I would of course try to keep my soul unblemished by not committing sinful acts.

Although I abandoned this childish notion that my soul looked like a transparent bone in the center of my body, the notion that I had a soul, like a belonging, stayed with me well into my adult life.

One day, as I was sitting with a friend, talking about spirituality, it dawned on me. "I don't have a soul – I am a spiritual being! I am a soul!" What a profound realization. I had spent the greater part of my life sitting in a fundamental confusion. I had settled on the idea that I had a soul and that my soul didn't really belong to me, it belonged to God. Can you imagine how life altering it was to realize that you are a spirit rather than have a spirit? At the moment of that realization, I felt something very profound and almost physical happen to me. My life would never be the same.

"All of us are here to go beyond our initial limitations, whatever they may be. We are here to recognize our magnificent and divine nature, regardless of what it may tell us."

Louise Hay

"If you grow what lies within you, what is within you will lead you to salvation. If you do not grow what lies within you, what fails to grow will destroy you."

Jesus Christ

"Put all your heart, your spirit, your mind and your soul into the smallest of your gestures. Such is the secret of success!"

Swami Sivanada

"What will it serve to win the world, if one should lose his soul in the process."

Blaise Pascal

"Man is a prison where the soul remains free."

Victor Hugo

"Consciousness is the light of intelligence to distinguish right from wrong."

Confucius

Déjà vu

I dreamt of life before
My soul traveled far and near
Death was but an opened door
The dream was all too clear

I remembered the battlefield
Facing ancestral foes
Clinging to sword and shield
Hearing the call of crows

I remembered America
On the sails of wooden ships
From the heart of Africa
Dry tongue on burning lips

I remembered child and wife
On Sunday afternoon
In some former life
As I gazed upon the moon

I dreamt of life before
Of all the parts I'd played
I could see there would be more
All from the bed I laid

"From the other side of tombs
Closed eyes still see."

Sully Prudhomme

It was a beautiful spring day as I walked with a close friend of mine. Ed and I would always wind up having a philosophical discussion about life and love.

"Look around you! Not everything you see is material in nature. Look at a beautiful sunset. It is partly material and partly ephemeral in nature" explained Ed.

"Well one can say that everything about the sunset is material, including the sun, the light and how the light hits the atmosphere. Even my ability to see it with my own eye is a material phenomena. However, my appreciation of the beauty of the sunset is definitely not material in nature," I responded.

As we walked, I began to see and experience how material and non-material forces mingled together

to form life itself. The birds, the trees, the flowers and all the living creatures were animated with a life force that was not material in nature.

In my own mind, a large part of livingness could not be reduced to a material manifestation like electricity or wave lengths. Some other phenomena was at work here giving life and form, guiding, creating harmony and even providing a mission for each thing. Underlying matter was intelligent movement.

At once, I began to see the magic in life. I began to see and experience something like a spiritual glue that put things together and made them work.

For some strange reason, I no longer felt alone but rather, I felt a deep kinship with all living things.

M. A.

"Love does not see with eyes but with the soul"

William Shakespeare

"Nothing is small for a great spirit."

Arthur Conan Doyle

Centuries of Belief

When we study religious and spiritual doctrines, we come to realize that they all share a number of common elements: the belief in a higher power or life force that we must attempt to know; a moral code of conduct to guide the individual in life and in with respect to others; the fundamental premise that man is not an animal, man is a spiritual being on a quest to discover the true nature of his spirit.

Since the beginning, man has inquired into his true nature. He has sought to understand and know the true meaning of life. The Veda, the holy book of the Hindus, written 1,800 years before Christ, attests to this fact. Whether we speak of Zen Buddhism, Taoism, Judaism or Christianity, we are always confronted with the same quest to know the spirit of man and man's place in the universe.

Religious and spiritual doctrines are important because they allow us to tend to our spirit. These doctrines must be protected as must the freedom of religious belief because it is the arena where man can strive to discover his true nature. In more recent years, efforts have been made to reduce the importance of religion and spiritual doctrine in the belief that science can better serve our needs. This idea is now being rejected more definitely as we realize that we need our connection to the world of spirit.

Above all, we realize that the true source of emotional and mental ills is spiritual in nature. Man's difficulties arise from the fact that he is a spirit within a body living within a material world that doesn't necessarily honor his true self. This fact alone justifies the existence and growth of religious and spiritual doctrine.

M. A.

"To thine own self be true
And it shall follow, as the night the day
Thou canst not then be false to any man."

William Shakespeare

"Great spirits have will,
weak ones have hope."

Chinese Proverb

"What we create within ourselves is always
reflected on the outside. Such is the law
of the universe."

Shakti Gawain

"Over time, I have learned that I must put
all my focus on inner knowledge. I have
realized that the greatest truth is what I come
to know from my own experiences, my senses
and my intelligence. There is no more vital
or more obvious truth than that comes
from within."

Marc Alain

"Until you can accept yourself, you block
the way that leads to the growth you aspire
to reach. This growth comes from your heart.
Be kind to yourself."

Emmanuel

"No one can live his life solely for himself.
Thousands of strings tie us to our brothers;
intertwined in these strings, such as feelings
of compassion, our actions are transmuted
into causes and return to us as effects."

Herman Melville

"Giving money isn't enough. Money can
always be found. What the poor really need
is love from your heart. Spread love
wherever your path takes you!"

Mother Teresa

The Dance of Life

The seasons they dance
They dance their never-ending dance
And every day we join in
Towards our own never-ending

The smiles and kindness of today
Will be the flowers and milk of tomorrow
The trespasses of today
Will be the burdens of tomorrow

In our every action we build
We build the path that our feet travel
We build the prison that we fear
We build the freedom so desired

And as the seasons they dance
So do we
Dancing the dance of freedom
Or dancing the dance of glee

The Artisans of Joy

When my husband and I discovered we couldn't have children, we were completely shattered. I remember, as a child, I had made the decision, whether consciously or not, that I would be a mother when I grew up. In fact my whole life had been structured to marry and to have children. I saw myself as a wife and mother. My choice to marry Frank was based on the notion that he would make a great father for our kids.

When the doctor told us that I could not bear children for medical reasons, I sat there in disbelief. My whole world came crashing in on me. I cried for days and days. I'll admit that this experience was so devastating that I thought of ending it all. For me this was more than tragic; it was as if I no longer had a goal in life. I had lost my mission and had no reason to live.

During those months, Frank stood by me. He did everything he could think of to console me, without much success. He insisted that we should look at the possibility of adopting kids. But I just couldn't accept that option. My children had to come from within me. They had to be my children not someone else's.

Later on that year, just before Christmas, my younger brother Gerry and his fiancée Cynthia came to visit. At that time, Cynthia was working for the Children's Aid Society as a child-care worker. During dinner, Cynthia mentioned that the

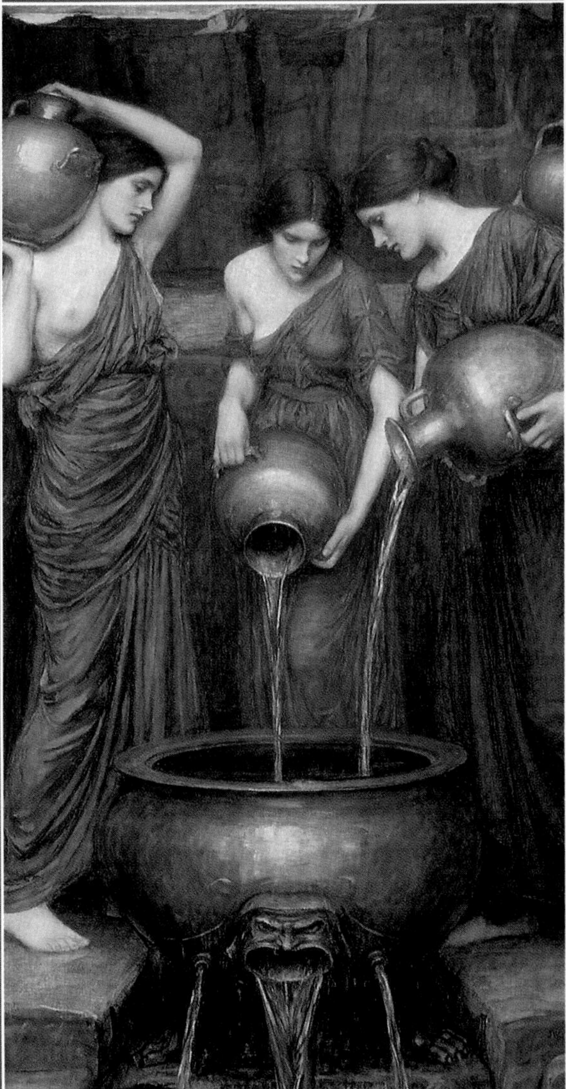

Children's Aid was having a lot of difficulty finding foster homes for all the kids. I asked her what was required to become a foster parent. She explained the basic requirements and gave me a number to call if I wanted to find out more.

After many discussions with Frank, we decided to try our hand at being foster parents. I'll admit that I was not at all prepared for the experience. Many of the kids we accepted into our home over the years were in pretty rough shape, coming from broken homes. Frank and I had to work very hard to adapt to this new lifestyle.

We've been foster parents for over twenty years now. We have experienced every emotion under the sun. But we really love the kids. Right now, we have a set of twins, Lilly and Marilyn, who are five years old; Thomas, a twelve-year-old, who spends a lot of time in front of the computer; and Sam, an eight-year-old, who is very sensitive and artistic in nature. I love these kids as if they were my own.

Frank and I are so busy raising these kids that we seldom have time to ourselves. I see the role of foster parent as a vocation, my real vocation in life. Sometimes I think of the fact that I cannot have kids and I feel a little sad. Then I turn and look at one of the kids whom we have taken in and see the good we are doing. In a way, God has helped me to turn a great tragedy into something good.

Helen H.

"You have every interest in discovering what your own needs are and finding the words to express them. As you reveal their extent, their nature and as you formulate the deprivations, the losses, the frailty and the talents linked to them, before your eyes you will see emerging an X-ray of yourself. You will see exactly what you are made of, what you really need, and what joy you would feel if your needs were finally met."

Daphne Rose Kingma

Cat's Tongues

Here a recipe I think you'll enjoy. To make a dozen cat's tongues you'll need

- $1/4$ cup/50 grams of powered sugar
- 1 egg
- $1/3$ cup/45 grams of flour

Mix in the sugar with the already beaten egg until the mixture is white and creamy. Then add the flour and mix until you get a smooth paste.

You'll need to lightly preheat a cookie sheet and butter it. Then, use a spoon to pour the mixture onto the cookie sheet in ribbons of $1/2$ inch by three or four inches. Then place in the preheated oven at 350°F/180°C until lightly brown. Enjoy.

"I came to realize that beyond all the things in life there were relationships. And these relationships provided the real food and sustenance of life."

Mark Blair

I was engaged to be married when I began to have a recurring dull pain in my arm. At first, I was sure I had overexerted myself doing some type of physical activity. However, over the weeks and months that followed, this diffuse pain appeared more frequently and visited other parts of my body. These bouts were also accompanied with feelings of fatigue and sometimes blurred vision.

Janet, my wife to be, and I were becoming more and more concerned about these symptoms so I went to the hospital for a series of tests. I explained to the doctor that I could feel totally fine for days on end and then I would be hampered by unusual pains in my arms, legs and in my back. I soon discovered that I had multiple sclerosis. MS is a degenerative disease of the nervous system that affects a great number of young adults. I was twenty-eight years old when I discovered I had MS.

I could live with the idea that I had a disease that would render me progressively less physically able. But I had some things I really wanted to accomplish, such as get married, have kids, be successful at my job. I wondered and worried about whether or not I would be able to achieve these very basic goals I had set for myself now. I was especially worried that Janet would not want to marry a man with such a serious illness.

Janet and I talked a lot. She shared all of her concerns. We met with the doctor and then a few specialists to find out more about MS. Nothing prevented us from having kids but dealing with everyday living might become a real challenge over time. There was, at present, no real cure for MS but there were various methods to control the disease and slow down its progression. Janet and I agreed to move ahead together, get married and have kids.

I don't mind telling you that dealing with MS is a real challenge. What most people take for granted requires major effort and determination for me. But I have a great life anyway. I have a wonderful wife, two beautiful daughters whom I adore. In many ways MS has forced me to focus on the really essential things in life: communication, family and home life. I cannot do all the things I would like to do, but I give myself totally to my family and to those activities I can do despite this illness.

Chris M.

"Solitude is to the spirit what diet is to
the body: deadly if done too long nevertheless
they are sometimes necessary."

Vauvenargues

"The tallest tree was born from a tiny seed.
The tall tower started with a handful of dirt."

Lao Tzu

"We are living links in the force of life that
moves about among us and plays within us,
around us, uniting the furthest depths of the
Earth with the highest stars in the sky."

Alan Chadwick

"I cherish my ideals and despite everything,
I continue to believe that people are
fundamentally good."

Anne Frank

"If a blind man helped a cripple to walk,
the two could go far."

Swedish Proverb

"You will know truth and truth
will set you free."

John 8:32

There are Laws

There are laws. Principles govern our lives here on Earth as we interact with other human beings. With every fiber of our beings, we seek to create beauty and harmony in our lives and the lives of others. We strive to achieve this objective naturally, given our fundamental nature.

But in our feverish race to achieve material success, the approval of others and financial security, we sometimes neglect to identify and adhere to the fundamental principles that contribute to happiness and beauty.

We can trust our ability to make the right choices and to become the ultimate masters of our destiny. By listening to ourselves and by applying higher rules of virtue and truth, we succeed in rising above the depths of the superficial world of appearances, toward greater self-determination and serenity.

By applying certain life principles, we can live in harmony with the forces that govern life on Earth and above. By living in harmony with higher principles, we embrace the strength of truth, beauty and simplicity and ultimately encounter less resistance and fewer defeats in our path to higher consciousness.

M. A.

no spirit is by definition an immaterial essence. It has been called
Vital", the soul; life force; the divine self, the true self and more rec
he inner child. Nevertheless there is broad agreement that the spirit e
und is distinct from the body and from the mind. In our hearts, we all
hat we are spirits and that our body is our vessel as we travel throug
on this earth. When something or someone speaks to us and reach
deeply, it reaches our very soul, our true inner self. Despite the e

ure of our genes, we know, without a doubt that above and beyon
material self there is our spirit, which is our true and lasting self.
book is about spirit. It is about the most noble and fundamental ess
f human being and life on earth. For life to exist, for creation to o
or change to manifest itself, it must be endowed with spirit. This be
also about you. The real you. The creative, thinking, dreaming, br